The Sweet Life

The Sweet Life

The Missing "Peace" to Living a Fearless Sweet Life

DR. BRIAN D. RHOADS

Print ISBN-13: 9798663474634
First Edition

Disclaimer

I have changed some names to protect certain individual's privacy. To maintain the anonymity of the individuals involved, I have changed some details. The information in this book was correct at the time of publication, but the author does not assume any liability for loss or damage caused by errors or omissions. These are my memories from my perspective, and I have tried to represent events as faithfully as possible. Some sample scenarios in this book are fictitious. Any similarity to actual persons, living or dead, is coincidental. The information provided in this book is designed to provide helpful information on the subjects discussed. The author and publisher disclaim any liability in connection with the use of this information.

I dedicate this book . . .
To the Battle of Perseverance because the reward is in the struggle.
To Hope and Courage as together we fight the battles of good reason.
To Time and Patience for bringing calmness and peace to my life.
To Peace . . . Because of you I am Fearless.

Table of Contents

Introduction

When telling stories, I have always preferred short and sweet rather than long and drawn out. This probably has to do with my attention span being way too short! Therefore, I want this message to be clear, concise, and simple . . . not complicated. I thought about what you might want or need versus what I want and what I need to say. Most, but not all, of this book is personal events from my own life. I've always hated when someone would give expert advice without ever really experiencing or understanding what I was going through. With that being said, I want to be as transparent as possible. Hopefully, this will allow us to connect, and for you to connect with someone else somewhere throughout the book.

So, here we go. If you could name or use one word to describe yourself what would it be? Fearful, Arrogant, Kind, Selfish, Enthusiastic, Miserable, Deceptive, Wise, Courageous, Honest . . . the list could go on and on. What one word would others use to describe you? What word would you identify with the people in your life? In this book, characters will be identified with descriptors not by name. So, let me be the first to introduce myself; my name is Fearless. I must be very honest with you; I have not always been Fearless. In fact, I, like a lot of you, have been Fearful many times in my life. As a matter of fact, I have been named all these words at some point in my life. Am I proud of it? Absolutely NOT! But if we are all honest with ourselves, I think you would agree that you have not always been your best either. Our names as well as the names of others in your life can change at any given time for better or worse depending on the circumstances or season of life that we are in.

Do you like uncomfortable questions? I do not. In fact, I really hate questions, but here is one to keep in the back of your mind when reading this book. Do you really know what you want in life? It is perfectly ok to say no because personally, I am still figuring this out. But what I can tell you is what I do not want, and sometimes that is just as important. I do not want Misery in my life, nor do I want Confusion, Chaos, Deception, or Control. I do not have the time or desire to devote my energy toward these people in my life. I honestly believe from my own experiences that people and trials are placed in our paths, so we can be prepared to go through whatever life presents. It does not mean that you must be vindictive or hate them, it just means that their chapter in your story is over.[1] God will allow us to forget the miracle that we thought we had to get to the next miracle that He is going to give us. So, do not be afraid to ask for Peace, Clarity, Wisdom, Hope, Courage, Direction, and last but not least . . . Faith.

I believe that you are about to read this book for one of two reasons. First, you either need or want something to change in your life.

Second, maybe, you just want a better, sweeter life. I can guarantee that while reading the chapters, some characteristic, personality, or part of the message will hit home. Not everything, but something. Therefore, when exploring this book, keep an open mind. I want you to simply replace the descriptive trait names with names that relate to your own life. Pay attention to the "Sugar Cubes" that you will find throughout the chapters. These are meant to spark deep thought within yourself. Furthermore, use the "Sweet Thoughts" at the end of the chapters to write individual notes as new ideas develop. Think of these ideas as what you would put in your own personal journal of your journey—the journey to the Sweet Life that has been waiting for you. Let's begin!

Be the change that you wish to see in the world.

—Mahatma Gandhi

One

THE CHANGE

*L*ife is not fair. Avoid the snare that it should be. Let us get this out of the way first and foremost. I have been told by many that I can be blunt at times. So please do not be offended when I tell you that life does not owe you anything. Stop falling into the victimization concept of how life passed you by and you did not get what you thought you were entitled to. It was supposed to happen, and it had to happen. It is just that simple. Once you learn to accept this is when the real change starts to happen.

In life, everything is impossible until you make it possible by having faith that it will be. Nevertheless, a lot of us do not have the answers and that is perfectly acceptable. This is not meant to discourage you in any way. It just is the way it is. . . this is the world that we live in. I only say this to challenge you in your thinking and your will to change. Only with this internal transformation will the true metamorphic process begin in all of us.

Several years ago, I sat in a little local breakfast spot to start my Saturday. Now, I do not know about you, but as I have gotten older, I really love the smell of bacon and eggs cooking, with coffee brewing in the surrounding air. As I sat in a corner, a couple walked in and sat at the table beside me. It was obvious that they were regulars, because everyone who walked in spoke and waved to them. They seemed to bring a smile and sense of light to the entire room. I was intrigued by their presence.

As I ate my breakfast, the older man asked me, "How are the eggs?"

I stated, "They were perfect! Not everyone can cook them like my mother used to without getting the center too hard."

He laughed and replied, "Yes indeed, they all cook them too fast and with the stove too hot. The key is the low temperature and not rushing the process."

As we continued our conversation, I could not help but watch his wife pour the hot water into her clear coffee mug and pick a little tea bag from the container. She carefully opened the package and removed the bag by the little string, placing the tea into the hot steaming water. As she moved the bag slowly up and down, I could start to see the water changing to a different color. The longer the tea bag sat, the darker the water got. As the tea finally got to her satisfaction, she added a little sugar. Since I often tend to lose focus, I was starting to get distracted from my conversation with her husband as I watched her. I also noticed the sweetener container had white, pink, yellow, and blue packages. Meanwhile, my waitress began to refill my glass of ice-cold sweet tea. My mind was spinning at this point because it hit me! The "Aha!" moment! Sweet Tea . . .

the life-changing epiphany had been before my eyes my entire life. I just could not see it due to the fact that I was so selfishly wrapped up in the world that I thought revolved around me.

Hot Water—The Puppeteer

So, the analogy hit me right in the face as I watched the couple drink their tea. The hot water represents the world that we live in. The world, like the hot water, can be so hot that it will burn you if you are not careful. It can leave scars and wounds from the burn. Furthermore, it can cause pain, which reminds us to possibly do a test run by sipping the tea before we take a big gulp.

In a way, our life pains are no different. Physical and psychological emotional pain is given to us to protect and teach us to not make the same mistakes in life. Think about a fire, for example. What happens when you touch fire? It burns! But you remember that you touched it and the next time you tend to be a little more cautious. Our life experiences are, in a way, just the same. Our life pains can be warning signs to not make the same mistakes over and over.

Tea—The Puppet

Do you remember when the little lady removed the tea bag from the package by the string? Well, that's humanity . . . you and me. Next question, have you ever felt like the world has you on a string like a puppet? I will be the first to admit that I most definitely have. In a way, if you are not careful, the world can toss and turn you however it wants. It can sway you to the left, right, up, or down. Your circumstances in anytime or moment of your life can be controlled by the world that we live. Masterfully, the world is the puppeteer and you are its puppet. It can control your thoughts and body actions by one swift movement of its own. The world will use its abilities in darkness if we are not aware of its capabilities. Have you ever seen shadow puppetry? "Well, shadow puppetry is an art form where cutout figures are held between a source of light and some sort of screen. Various effects can be achieved by the puppeteer moving the puppets within that light source."[1] Many times, we put on one face in the light while allowing darkness to put a shadow over the happiness that misery has brought with it.

So, the real question is—what happens when the tea is placed in the water? Are you changing your world or is the world changing you?

If you can honestly say that you are changing your world, then here is my next question. Are you changing your world for the better or for worse? Are you truly making a difference to those around you? What have you done to change the world?

Sugar Cubes:

> To improve is to change; to be
> perfect is to change often.
>
> —WINSTON CHURCHILL

Innocence

It has been said, "When not interfered with by outside influences, everything nature does is done with perfection."[2]

My family was presented with nature's Innocence nearly twenty-five years ago. While Innocence brings many health issues, she is considered angelic in her own way. Innocence brings enthusiasm and joy to us. She is pure and has no prejudice. Innocence sees people as they are and only wants to see the good in them. She gives the benefit of the doubt. Innocence speaks truth and is forgiving when most would hold grudges. She requires nothing but love in return. With hope and courage, protection is given to Innocence. She is contagious and changes her world by her existence. It is natural for her. She has not been conditioned by the world to turn her head and ignore what is going on around her. She embraces and loves everyone. There is a lot to learn from Innocence.

Have you ever allowed yourself to be conditioned by society? Do you act differently when around a certain crowd?

Now, I have been to many ballgames with Innocence in my lifetime, and we always have one harmless argument. She tends to cheer for both teams. It really does not matter what sport . . . basketball, baseball, football—oh, and let us not forget wrestling, her absolute favorite.

As a guy on the opposing team scores, she cannot wait to scream and cheer him on.

A guy strikes out on our team and she says, "That's ok, get them next time!"

I quickly tell her," Innocence, you can't cheer for the other team!"

She replies, "Why?"

With confusion on my face, I paused for a moment . . . "Because you can't cheer for two teams. You just don't."

Why? She had a point, you know. Why do we not cheer each other on? Why can we not speak when others walk by? Is this really what we have become? Have we become so distracted by our smartphones and other devices that we do not even notice those in the elevator beside us? Or . . . are we so self-absorbed in ourselves that we place little significance toward anyone else?

Here is a thought. We simply do not place connections as a priority in our lives. Some do not even know how to connect. We selfishly care only about ourselves. While connections bring various relationships to our lives, many never experience true connections. Genuine connections allow us to see one another as we are. Only when a true desire for connections has developed will we begin to realize that we cannot do it alone and are stronger together.

Protocol

I have been in dentistry now for over twenty-two years. When away from my dental practice, I have the privilege of teaching third- and fourth-year dental students at a university. A few weeks ago, one of my novice students, named Protocol, excitedly approached me to obtain approval to begin his appointment. As part of the normal process required, he proceeded to tell me the entire medical history of his patient.

With much enthusiasm, he said, "I have a fifty-six-year-old Black female with a history of high blood pressure and an allergy to penicillin. She is a new patient and seems to be extremely nervous. Today we are doing a treatment plan!"

As I listened, I stared at him for a moment before I replied. Then with a half-cocked smirk on my face, I said, "Great, now tell me something about your patient."

I could tell by Protocol's face that he was now confused. I knew what he was thinking; I had been there before. He was thinking, "Can he not hear? I just told him about her."

With a bold voice, Protocol repeated, "She is fifty-six years old, has high blood pressure, and an allergy to penicillin!"

I quickly replied, "I heard you the first time. Now tell me something about your patient. Does she sew? How many grandchildren does she have? How long has she lived here? I want you to connect with your patient."

I am sure that by this point, Protocol's look of complete confusion and aggravation could be felt on the entire floor. I mean come on, what is the big deal? Let the guy just work on her teeth, right?

Protocol's next response was just as I thought it would be—as it is many times when "green" students enter the clinical phase of their matriculation through school.

"How?" he replies. "What do I say?"

I looked up slowly and said, "I want you to truly meet your patient. She is a person not a case. How many grandchildren does she have? Where is she from? What kind of ice-cream does she like? Just talk to her."

As time went by, I continued to check on the other students. I turned the corner and there stood Protocol with a smile like he had just won the lottery. He said, "She likes strawberry, Doc! Strawberry!"

As I looked down at his patient, we all three laughed out loud. I said, "Good job, bud, good job!"

Hopefully, you have gathered that this really has nothing to do with ice-cream or becoming a dentist. My instructions to Protocol were given so that he might learn to connect with his patients.

Connection versus Relationships

Human connection works when we are open with one another, allowing a sense of trust to develop. It will only continue to build when we consistently bring honesty to the table. When we connect with someone, we live in the moment by sharing experiences together. This allows us to develop more empathy and kindness toward one another.[3] Thus, creating a better atmosphere regardless of whether they are strangers or not.

Many people search for the relationship connection. Meaning, they look for the relationship first rather than trying to connect with someone. Relationships need time—to see if they will evolve or not and whether they are a good fit for you. Some people simply hide certain truths about themselves, to create an illusion, by camouflaging their weaknesses. Strategy becomes the main objective which causes extreme difficulty in a real connection ever developing.[4]

Searching endlessly for the relationship first, prior to waiting for the connection to evolve, destroys the chance of the relationship ever developing. Trying to sell yourself before an attempt to truly bond, keeps you from ever finding the true loyalty that comes from long-lasting relationships that might develop. Leading one on by playing games hinders you from being transparent, while trying to anticipate your next move. How can you expect the relationship to evolve when all you have done is to show a false misrepresentation of yourself?

Have you ever put the relationship search first? Have you ever been in a relationship where you felt disconnection? How can we successfully connect with each other?

First, if you, the tea, are to change your world, you must be honest without an angle. You must be transparent and open minded with no agenda. Second, attempt to be the best authentic version of yourself that you possibly can be. Strive to be better today than you were yesterday. By doing this, you will inadvertently learn how to connect with yourself. Connecting with yourself enables you to love yourself. Realizing that you are not perfect shines a new light that no one else is either. Being vulnerable allows connections to develop at its best while all walls of falsehood have been torn down. Third, you must see the imperfect real me before you can respect me. However, I must see the imperfect real you before I can fully respect you. We must see each other before we can learn to respect each other.

A successful relationship requires teamwork. Couples and teammates must put in consistent effort and time if they wish to get desirable results. Great relationships do not just magically appear because of the initial love that you had when you first met. How well you consistently build love through the trials and efforts of your hard work is what will matter in the end. Therefore, a person who gives more than they take will never have to worry about loyalty.

While connection is evolving, do not confuse compatibility with chemistry. Webster states, "Relationship compatibility exists when a couple relates with equality and respect. It is important for couples to have fun together and really enjoy the time that they spend together. Relationships thrive when two people share companionship and activities."[5]

Chemistry, on the other hand, involves a reaction or change between two substances or people. Do you remember your chemistry class in high school? What happened when you mixed two substances together? If mixed under the correct conditions, these combinations can transform into something of a positive nature. However, together they also change to a completely different state than their true original form. Other times, the two substances or people just do not mix at all. Maybe, one settles on the bottom while the other is suspended. Furthermore, the molecules repel each other if the attraction is not there—such as oil and water. The mixture or relationship can even become toxic with detrimental effects. As conditions, such as a heated environment, develop in this experimental situation, an explosion can and will occur if left together for too long. Sometimes people can have a greater purpose and better qualities when left alone. It does not mean that they are bad people at all. It just simply means that they are not a good fit for each other.

There was a time in my life that I found myself guilty of confusing chemistry with compatibility. We lacked respect for each other and did not desire the same qualities in a person. Initial chemistry and attraction presented themselves, but also came in the form of lust and greed. When characteristics of these sorts are chosen above all else, the chemical relationship will fail. Instead, make a conscious effort to choose qualities that have value when searching for a compatible connection. Pick qualities such as integrity, determination, and dependability over deceitfulness, control, and greed.

About three years ago, I went to buy my son a used car. After driving several cars, we finally settled upon a red Dodge Challenger.

The salesman said, "Well, what do you think?" I carefully replied, "What is the history?" Now I have learned over the years that not everyone takes care of their car like I do. Therefore, I always check the Carfax. For those of you who do not know, the Carfax is basically a background check of the vehicle. It will tell you everything about the car. Where it is from. Has it been wrecked? Are there any insurance claims? You get the picture. However, occasionally something can be missed. Maybe the owner sold or traded it in prior to the information being recorded soon enough. In this case, the new buyer would never know the damage until it is too late.

Wouldn't it be nice if we could get the same type of instant report on people before we bring them into our lives? We could call it something catchy like "The Gold Digger Report" or even possibly "The Loser Chart." We could find out their negative habits, personality type, and obvious motives. If they do not meet our criteria, then hit the road, Jack! Man, would this not prevent a lot of useless time, grief, and heartache. Okay, so I know this is unrealistic, but here is the point. Before letting a possible friend, significant other, or business partner edge into your life, ask yourself some reflective, tough questions. Questions like—what does this person want from me?

Does this person have my best interest as a priority? What do my family members and friends think about them? Is this person using me?

While doing this, do not get caught in a trap of mimicry. An example of mimicry would be the Monarch and Viceroy butterflies. Basically, one is poisonous and the other is not, but they resemble each other. This resemblance or copy catting allows the Viceroy to protect itself from its predatory environment.[6] This proves that sometimes what you see is not always what you get. Do not get caught in the trap of mimicry by choosing someone disguised with deceptive, miserable, or chaotic characteristics. The kind of people that you surround yourself with says a lot about you.

Therefore, when asking questions, do not forget to listen. Then, when you think you are listening, listen again. Take note that we have two ears and only one mouth for a reason. So, you listen twice as much as you speak. By listening, it will be easier to identify compatible, fun interests and long-term goals that exist between each other. Thereby leading to less heartache, grief, and disappointment that could follow.

Sugar Cubes:

> Everyone thinks about changing the world,
> but no one thinks of changing himself.

—LEO TOLSTOY

Sweet Thoughts:

_____

_____

_____

_____

_____

_____

_____

_____

_____

_____

_____

_____

_____

_____

_____

_____

_____

_____

_____

_____

_____

_____

_____

_____

_____

_____

"When it is all finished you will
see it was never random."

—KAREN SALMANSOHN

Two

ICE

In 1972, a thin, tall lanky basketball player named George Gervin entered the American Basketball Association (ABA), a rival league to the National Basketball Association (NBA). He was smooth as silk as he moved graciously around the court. His signature move to the basket was his famous rain-maker finger roll. He possessed a rare ability to perform at a high level without sweating. As people noticed his cool play and calm demeanor on the court, he was rightfully given the nickname "The Iceman."

Who are the teammates in your life? Better yet, who can you count on when the game is on the line? Life is a team sport much like basketball. Hope and Courage are the guards of my life. Clarity, Wisdom, and Direction are my forwards because that is the way I have decided to move . . . Forward. Belief is the center of my team—believing that it does not matter if we win or lose, but how we play the game. Inspiration is my reserve, as he knows to step in when fatigue and doubt begin to develop. Peace is the team cheerleader, giving us the push to finish what we started. Last, but not least, Faith is the captain of my team, as He always knows when to show up and on time.

Faith is the calm, cool, and most important ingredient to making life the sweetest. With Faith, you never sweat under pressure. Faith allows you to have complete trust that everything is going be alright. Although he can easily be lost, he eagerly waits to be found. He brings a sense of coolness and confidence when situations are tense. Faith is believing when you have nothing left. He will give you the hope and courage needed to feel invincible. Faith gives direction while staying the course. He will provide wisdom and clarity when making prayerful decisions. Faith makes you fearless and brings peace to your life.

Icebergs

Several years ago, I decided to take my family on an Alaskan cruise. Each day we would wake up to a different location of beautiful landscape and scenery. One early morning, I managed to get up before my family as well as most of the other passengers. As I walked out onto the empty deck, the cold air took me by surprise. I realized that we were sitting right in the middle of Glacier Bay National Park. My daughter must have heard me leave the room as she was now standing beside me. The clean air felt so refreshing, but the silence is what I can never forget. The calm waters were slick as glass, with hues and shades of blue beyond the color scale. There was extraordinarily little conversation as we both stood in awe of nature's beauty. Slowly, we started to hear little pops and crackling as small pieces of ice started to fall off the glacier into the water below. The crackling intensified, sounding like thunder pounding in the sky. Suddenly, an enormous piece of ice broke free, splashing into the freezing waters. Waves quickly developed, pushing and shoving the boat in an irregular motion. Both of our eyes now widened; we looked at each other speechless.

Icebergs form when pieces or chunks of ice break off from larger glaciers. They travel by ocean currents, many times getting trapped and smashed against the shoreline in the shallow waters. When the broken ice reaches warmer temperature, it is attacked from all sides. This causes the iceberg to melt in certain spots, creating "melting ponds" that seep through, therefore widening the cracks. As little particles continue to separate, eventually stress causes more chunks to break free, creating smaller bergs called growlers and bits. These can be considerably dangerous for ships because they are more difficult to spot in treacherous waters.[1]

In comparison, our problems are remarkably like the formation of icebergs. Problems that come with misery, deception, and chaos build upon one another as they break free from their source. They can change with their environment, just as the ice vanishes into the melting ponds. Time and patience reveal that they still exist, only they have transformed into a different shape or form. Many times, the problems that we see are only, in essence, "the tip of the iceberg."[2] In correlation, much like the glacier, there usually is a larger problem that lies beneath the surface. Without a watchful eye, the large seasonal problems that come from time to time will cause us to eventually sink. Seasons, meaning life changes and letdowns, which simply come with time and age . . . such as a midlife crisis, for example.

How do you identify problems or icebergs before they cause damage to your ship? You must know your current coordinates. Where you have been. Where you are. Where you are going. Without a plan or direction, solutions that are needed to solve problems will be near impossible.

Sugar Cubes:

> "The pessimist complains about the
> wind, the optimist expects it to change,
> the realist adjusts the sails."
>
> —WILLIAM ARTHUR WARD

The GPS

I love to fish. There is just something so magical about being on the calm glass-like surface early in the morning. The water seems so alive as the ripples start to develop across its surface. Although I do not always catch fish, I seem to come back with a better sense of direction and appreciation than when I started.

A couple of months ago, a friend of mine named Direction asked me to go kayak fishing with him. Although I had been to this lake before, it had been many years ago since I had been there. Like we all do nowadays, my buddy and I put the address in our phones to take us to the correct location. As we looked at the navigation system—the Global Positioning System (GPS)—we could see the blue landmark on the screen indicating that we were getting close to the water.

The voice on our phone continued to prompt us on our next turn, and I looked over at Direction and said, "This doesn't feel right."

Direction replied, "What do you mean? She said turn back there." I had been here before, but everything looked different and it just did not feel right. So, I decided to take matters into my own hands and turn at the next road.

We continued to drive for a couple miles, while continuously listening to the voice telling us to make a U-turn as she routed us with new directions. At this point, Direction looked at me and said, "Do you think maybe she was right in the beginning?" After passing a guy riding his bike, I decided to stop and ask him for directions, which absolutely killed me inside. Come on, you know men never ask for directions!

He said, "You're lost, aren't you?"

I said, "How did you know?"

He replied with a soft laugh and a smirk, "Because you passed me three times."

As Direction and I listened closely for instructions, we started to laugh at one another. We quickly realized that yes, the voice was correct the entire time. Even though she was giving us the proper directions to reach the lake, I had not trusted her . . . . It did not feel right. I simply wanted to do it my way.

Isn't this the way that we live our own lives?

Think about it. The Ice, our calm and cool, gives us a clear path to follow, yet in our own arrogance we want to do it our own way. Basically, we think that we are so smart and that our intelligence will provide us with a better plan for handling things. Then when situations get too hot for us to handle, we start searching for our calm and cool "Iceman" to come in and save the day. People fail to recognize that the correct path never changes . . . WE change. At times, we are going to be required to make U-turns in our lives to get us back on track. Other times, you may come to a crossroads and will have to make some difficult decisions.

Will you take that road less traveled or the broad road that society has made for you?

The Road Not Taken

"Two Roads diverged in a wood, and
I took the one less traveled by,
And that has made all the difference."[3]

—ROBERT FROST

There is a big difference in what one wants versus what one does not want. It is also important in knowing the difference in focusing your energy on what you did not do versus what you did do. I love this piece from Robert Frost's, "The Road Not Taken." To me, it means taking chances and not following the decisions and expectations that society has already made for you. It's about following your heart and having the guts to do what you and only you want to do with no regrets. However, don't get caught up with the question, "How did I get here?" and the letdowns that come in life of what you did not do.[4] Instead, battle that mentality with the positive energy of what you did do.

Direction

When one finds Direction, he feels strong in the guidance that comes with him. He is consistently by your side and will assist you in finding your way. Direction holds you account- able, enabling you to stay the course. He does not look back and has a motivating purpose. Although you can lose your way, Direction helps you in the endless search to finding yourself. He allows him- self to slow down and look for the road signs that give advice. While Direction can see the warnings and hazards that lie ahead, he will take the necessary detours to protect you from the wrong turns that deception, misery, and chaos bring with them. Direction's aim is moving forward and Faith travels with him.

What wrong turns and choices have you made in your life that you wish you could change? Or have you ever been going in the right direction only to be detoured by making the wrong decision?

Skid Marks . . . No Pun Intended

Know when to leave "Skid Marks." Yeah, that is what I said. I thought you might need a little humor. We might as well laugh about it. For those of you who still do not get it, these are the

"Oh no!" moments or decisions that you make that come back to haunt you. I get it . . . . Your mind and thoughts were going at warp speed and you wanted instant gratification. Give yourself a little credit because you did think about hitting the brakes for a moment. However, you indeed decided not to hit the brakes and think before you made the turn. You still impulsively reacted and made the decision anyway. These are the Skid Marks I am talking about. If you would have pumped the brakes and thought about the long-term effects of your decision, these Skid Marks could have saved you a lot of grief.

For example, your utility bill is passed the due date. You borrowed $250 from the petty cash box at work without asking. You forget to put it back. Now, your boss is asking questions. Oh no!

Maybe, you go out on a "harmless" date, as you call it. To later find out the guy that you are now talking to works with your boyfriend or spouse.

Say you had one too many drinks at the game last night. You are hung over and feel awful, but you must teach Sunday school this morning.

The stories could go on and on, but regardless, these are all Skid Marks that you should have made. No pun intended, but these are the tracks that are left behind before making those wrong turns. The lack of Skid Marks causes you to constantly look in your rearview mirror, which causes you to look back, preventing progress in moving forward. They cause stress and come in the form of guilt and regret. The downhill speed at which you are going becomes dangerously out of control. Failing to pump the brakes will possibly cause you to crash and burn. Your distance becomes further and further from the destination and location that you had planned on going to. The feeling of remorse starts to set in as the light at the end of the tunnel seems so dim.

When driving down the highway you, on occasion, put the car on cruise control, right? However, once the road starts to develop hills and curves, you must slow down and pump the brakes. Now add the fact that it is getting dark and traffic is thickening by the moment. It is starting to rain and the headlights from oncoming vehicles are bright and blinding. Think about how difficult it would be to stay on your side of the road without having boundaries? Envision these yellow lines as the lanes or rules that society requires us to live by. They aim to bring order and protection to our shared world. Guardrails, on the other hand, are a very personal set of boundaries. They are the accountability rules that we set for ourselves. These rules are not enforced by anyone other than you. Therefore, these individualized guardrails usually involve integrity, morals, and ethics. Setting boundaries in combination with Skid Marks provide protection when losing focus. Now let us go a step further. Say you did manage to lose focus and surprisingly got blindsided. Uncharacteristically, you made a poor decision and failed to hit the brakes. You lost control, slid off the road, and landed in a ditch. With little success, you try to back up in reverse, but are now stuck in a mound of mud. As panic sets in, you continuously spin your wheels, which only causes you to sink further and further. You finally realize that you need help.

Knowing when to swallow your pride and ask for help involves humility. When people come to your rescue, recognize their presence, as these are the proven individuals that you can always count on to provide direction. When driving down unfamiliar territory, it is necessary to practice caution. Avoid dead-end roads that do not have predictable escape routes. Learn to recognize and avoid the situations that cause you to cross your guardrails. Road conditions or, better yet, life temptations can become treacherous at any given moment. Slowing down allows you to make decisions that are more desirable in reaching your destination. Even the best of drivers can have a life-damaging accident without guardrails or boundaries put in place. Everyone can make a bad decision or mistake under certain conditions. So, when you do cross the guardrail or fail to pump the brakes, do not beat yourself up over it. Make it right, and then leave the past in the past. Instead of pondering over your letdowns, you must blaze a new trail. Today, tomorrow, and the days ahead are where your focus should be. That is where you will find life to be the fullest. In other words, do not look back.

Sugar Cubes:

> Boundaries don't keep other people
> out; they fence you in.
>
> —PICTUREQUOTES.COM

I bet right now you are saying, "I've made so many mistakes!" What now?

Have you ever thought about why the rearview mirror in your car is so small while the windshield is like a hundred times bigger? Because it is more important to be aware of where you are going then where you have been. The mistakes and marks that are BEHIND us are simply that . . . . Behind us. The further we get from the marks we created, the smaller they become in our rearview mirror.[5] While they 100 percent tell the story of where we have been, they are not the final stop of our journey.

Sugar Cubes:

There are unknown forces that truly do not want us to know what we are capable of. They do not want us to know the extraordinary things that we believe in ourselves are real. We give each other permission to say and do whatever we want by the cowardice of our lies and actions. By living in the shadows of one's identity, they find it is difficult to hold onto the light. These people who do not want others to know the truth today they lose.[6,7]

Sweet Thoughts:

Hope is wishing it would happen,
Belief is knowing it will happen,
Courage is making it happen.

—B. Rhoads

Three

PURE SWEETNESS

I was a young twenty-three-year-old and in my last year of finishing my doctorate when I found out that my wife was pregnant with my son. I so vividly remember pulling into the driveway and seeing my wife and mother-in-law sitting overly concerned on the front porch.

I asked, "What's going on?"

My wife hesitantly replied, "I'm pregnant!"

What? This could not be happening right now. This was not part of my plan. My hesitation seemed like an eternity, but let me tell you, at that moment time stood still.

Now let me ask you, have you ever said something that you wish you could take back? I most certainly have and here was my time. Open mouth, insert foot, and, before I knew it, I said it.

"Well that's just freaking great!!" I rudely replied. "I've spent all day with Dr. Terror, and you tell me you're pregnant! How did this happen?" I knew exactly what had caused it, but why now? Now was not the time, I thought.

As my wife frantically ran into the house crying, my mother-in-law quickly said, "You're a real jerk!"

Yeah, she was right . . . .

It was probably not my best moment. If I had it to do all over again, I would have chosen my words a little better . . . I hope!

Hope

Hope? There is a word. Have you ever lost hope? Has hope ever been your saving grace? What is Hope to you?

Hope is the positive mentality that everything is going to be alright. He is by your side when you feel like you have nothing left. Hope will team with Courage in conquering any obstacle in their way. He is a freelancer and can disappear when discouraged but will find you in times of despair. He has a mind of his own and is not easily figured out. Hope needs a cause worth fighting for. He brings promise and optimism that he can change his world. Hope brings possibility to reality. Therefore, he wants to see the best in you. In desperate times, Hope is the knot at the end of your rope. He puts life in perspective while building enough courage to rise up! Furthermore, Hope gives the vision that tomorrow is a new day. "Hope walks through the fire while Faith leaps over it."[1]

Courage

Let me say that if Hope is currently in your life, Courage will need to follow soon. While Hope takes time, Courage is swift and takes immediate action. Courage takes Hope as inspiration in connecting with fearlessness. Courage has mental toughness and a desire to confront intimidation. She is deliberate in her action and nothing is by accident. Her abilities and thinking bring confidence. She will fight for the cause with little care of winning or losing. Courage does not run away even when presented with the impossible; because the impossible does not exist in her eyes. Courage takes care of her own while protecting her name. She knows how to give mercy, but only if you have earned it. Courage is silent when silence is required. She will not quit in the face of failure but uses it to conquer her next battle. Courage and Hope will bring the Peace that you pray for. Courage finishes her battle and says, "Who is next?"

Sweetness! Pure sugar! Only you can define your own sweetness in your life. You can make it as sweet as you like it. For example, Hope and Courage are my sweetness. So, are my family, my friends, fishing, working out, and traveling, to name a few. We all determine what makes life worthwhile. What is it that brings happiness to your life? Have you ever really thought about it?

Studies show that sugar or sweetness has the highest taste recognition on our taste buds, while bitter has the lowest. It is now known that not only are sweet taste receptors found on the tongue but also in your gastrointestinal (GI)tract. These triggers also participate in controlling your feeling of hunger. Ironically, it is difficult to satisfy this hunger once we have tasted it.[2]

However, our sweetness is so much more than the tangible. Think about it for a second. What about acceptance, confidence, security, love, health, forgiveness, and let us not forget, second chances? Although I cannot physically touch or visually see these characteristics, they indeed bring immeasurable sweetness to my life.

I Believe in You

Belief may be one of the most unappreciated influential words in our vocabulary. While Belief is a noun, Believe is a verb. Let me explain. Belief is the state of something that a person deems true. On the other hand, Believing requires action in accepting the truth or self-assurance that a certain result will occur.

What happens when someone believes in you? Better yet, what happens when you believe in someone?

When someone genuinely believes in you, the feeling is contagious. Everything begins to change. Hope and Courage start to empower you by their pure existence. Fearlessness and confidence start to build, making the impossibilities laughable.

In times of doubt, Hope and Courage will rise to the occasion when a strong sense of Belief is present. Belief comes with a cause and gives us the push to do more. She gives you the will to fight your battle with heart and purpose. Her focus is on the fight not the fright. Belief's inspiration is driven by the Hope- and Courage-filled moment. She will help you see your most positive qualities and utilize those to the fullest. Belief helps you to see the best in yourself when you cannot. She gives you a platform to constantly say "I can!" Believing finds the Faith that you had given up on, which brings confidence that you actually were never alone.

Have you ever stopped believing in yourself? What do you do when you lose focus and belief?

There was a time in my life when I was truly angry and lost. I had just turned forty, staring middle age in the face. I gradually started losing my identity as I struggled with the loss of my father. I had worked my entire life for his approval and advice. His words of affirmation that I had always longed for would never happen. He was gone in the blink of an eye. The torch had been passed, and I was not ready to accept it. I became bitter as my frustrations grew by the day.

Moreover, I had come to grasp and accepted that I had placed myself in another toxic relationship. I was considered successful in society's eyes, but this success was not enough for me. I continued to put on my daily happy face, but inside I was miserable. I had concluded that enough was enough and started having unhealthy damaging thoughts. I would drive around cursing my life while developing the "Why me?" mentality. Then one night it came . . . . I wanted to talk with my dad. I had questions and I was going to get answers one way or another. I do not remember getting out of my truck, but I could feel the cold air and rain hitting my skin. The ground was wet as I crawled down on my knees to feel my dad's headstone. My mind had finally succumbed to the emotional stress and pushed me to my limit. At that moment, I realized that I was six feet from the edge and falling. My fingertips were freezing as I held the cold black steel in one hand and touched the name on the stone with the other. I had never been this desperate and always seemed to have it together. What was I to do? It seemed like hours went by as I cried out loud and wrestled with my emotions. Empty, I concluded that prayer was all I had left. As I continued to feel the sensation of cold rain on my now wet body, I screamed for help in my desperation. Silence! I was still alone, so I thought. Goosebumps started to develop as I felt two hands touch my shoulders. As I slowly opened my eyes, I looked to my left and there stood Hope. I then looked to my right side and I found Courage staring back at me. I will never forget their soft-spoken words, "Let's go home, Dad, let's go home."

With a combination of fear and sweet relief, I knew the spontaneous presence of Hope and Courage was not by accident. Although I had temporarily lost belief in myself, they gave me the will to get up in the final seconds of the tenth round. We will not choose devastation and surrender. Through perseverance, we realize that by falling down seven times, we stand up eight. Standing up again and again until the final bell rings.

Do you believe in someone? Have you ever said the words, "I believe in you?"

Dear Fearless,

It has been a crazy few weeks. It has put a lot of pressure on our family and our faith in God. We have all learned a lot about our family in the process (some good, some not so good). But I wrote you this to tell you how much I love and appreciate you. Somehow, through all the struggles we have faced recently, you've managed to be supportive of us through it all. Family has been put as your priority (after God of course). Although you have broken down along the way, you always pull yourself back together. I hope that you know that I've always got your back. Even though you are older than me, you can always depend on me to take control of the situation. It has been hard lately to stay focused and positive. We've both wanted to give up, but we have too many people depending on us. You have changed more in the past month than I have ever seen (for the better). You have become a better man. If things work out, great; if not we've got this. Regardless of the outcome, we have gotten stronger together. Thank you for sacrificing your time, energy, money, and happiness just for us to have a better life. Thank you for being selfless even during the times that I have been selfish. I hope this brings a little bit of happiness to you because I love you so much.

Courage

Do not let your life pass by without delivering those powerful words, "I believe in you" to someone whom you love. On that cold rainy night at the grave site of my father, I learned a valuable lesson. Hope and Courage are the sleeping giants that live within all of us. When awakened by the slightest bit of Faith, we start to develop the roar and heart of a lion. By knowing that we are not alone, we can face and acknowledge our fears. I have confidence that Hope, and Courage believe in me. On the other hand, they need to know that I believe in them. As a result, we can defeat anything that comes our way. Together we live what we believe. That, my friends, is why Belief is priceless.

Knowing that Hope and Courage were on my side gave me a new sense of power. I started to focus on the positive by pouring as much sweetness into my life as I could. I began my mornings with motivational podcasts and YouTube segments while getting ready for the day. I listened to successful speakers such as Les Brown, Zig Ziglar, Tony Robbins, and John Maxwell. I found that starting my day with a strong positive attitude was not only empowering for me but also contagious to those around me. I began to understand that seasonal uphill struggles are inevitable. Thus, I accepted the fact that sometimes the reward is the struggle. With this growth mindset, I made a personal decision that I would strive to move forward while attempting to balance my life. John Maxwell couldn't have said it better, "Everything worthwhile is all uphill. We have high uphill hopes with downhill habits."[3] To meet the level of success that I had dreamed of, I first had to define where I was going and accept where I was currently. This reality check forced me into a new philosophy of balance and equilibration.

Balance

My life can basically be broken down into five major categories: family, faith, work, friends, and health. Maybe your life categories are different from mine. Regardless, I find that it is necessary to self-evaluate from time to time. Sometimes you may be so engulfed in your job that you neglect your significant other by postponing date night. You decide to skip your son or daughter's ballgame to go out with coworkers. As luck would have it, you missed their first homerun. Other times, you are so involved with your family that you put off your friends. It has been weeks, maybe months, since you have talked to them. You later find out that one of them has been in the hospital. Maybe you skip church to workout. The list could go on and on, but an even distribution of your time and energy should be of priority when striving for life balance. It is inevitable that your balance list will categorically change. Therefore, consistent effort and evaluation is necessary to avoid tipping the scales.

While I strive to fill my life with sweetness, I find it imperative to surround myself with those that have the same positive outlook. I desire to surround myself with people—where we both believe in each other. In turn, we both strive to make sure our relationship is sustainable. There is an old saying, "If you lie with dogs, you'll end up with fleas." Do not be with parasites that attach and suck the happiness out of your life. Associating with destructive people will leave you with a negative attitude. Do not let negative words lead to adverse thoughts. Follow people who use positive action and reinforcement words in their way of thinking and speaking. Look for those people who can enrich your life. When hiring a workout trainer, do you want someone who is not physically fit? When you go to your dentist, do you want him or her to have an unpleasant smile and decaying teeth? No, you want to be around people that practice what they preach. Being with like-minded people allows you to challenge one another with diversified thinking. Furthermore, be inspired and motivated by one another as you press forward through your failures and successes.

Developing a health strategy is necessary, whether we like it or not. Suppressive negative attitudes leads to less energy, which leads to even more negative thoughts and feelings. Exercise allows me to personally escape and vent from the negative aspects of my life. The rewards of less stress and better health give a more optimistic confident outlook when problems present themselves. You must take care of yourself first. If you do not, then who will?

While taking care of your body, do not forget to include your mind and soul. Experiment by trying new hobbies and leisure activities when searching for the sweet spot of your life. These pastimes help you relax from the daily worries and anxiety that life brings. Social connections with friends and family also bring positive results. Learn to travel and see the world. Maybe you like fishing, hiking, bicycling, spending time with your kids, reading a book. Resourcing yourself with pleasurable stress-free actions will give you a feeling of rejuvenation and is like a breath of fresh air.

Sugar Cubes:

> You cannot truly know the sweetness of great
> joy without the bitterness of great sorrow.
>
> —JEFFREY FRY

Sweet Thoughts:

_____

_____

_____

_____

_____

_____

_____

_____

_____

_____

_____

_____

_____

_____

_____

_____

_____

_____

_____

_____

_____

_____

_____

_____

_____

_____

_____

_____

_____

Remember the sweetness that exists
when life throws you a lemon.
Together, they make lemonade.

—B. Rhoads

Four

The Lemon

$\mathcal{M}$y dad was a Chevy man. I do not really know why except that my grandfather was a Chevy man, as well as my uncle. It is just in our blood. So, what would you guess that I am? You got it . . . a Chevy man. I will never forget the time that my mother needed a new car and insisted that my father try a Ford for a change. I can remember countless conversations at the dinner table, debating over the vehicle. Until one day, my dad got so tired of this discussion that he reluctantly agreed to go take a look. It was a normal sunny Saturday and, as usual, I was playing basketball in the driveway with friends. Suddenly, my parents pull up in a Gold Ford Explorer. What just happened? Had my dad been hypnotized? He would put his hand in a blender before he would ever consider buying a Ford!

Well, indeed he did. For the next month, all I heard was how my dad hated this car and what a mistake he had made. He went against his own better judgment. My mother would call at least once a day with a problem. "The red engine light is on, tire pressure is being lost, the AC will not work, and there is a noise." You get the point! Out of pure frustration, he would shout," FORD . . . stands for Fix or Repair Daily!"

After several weeks of grief, my parents decided to return the car to the dealership. After a long debate, it was determined by all parties to deem the vehicle a "Lemon."

Those of you who are not familiar with this definition, let me explain. Lemon is a term in the car industry that is used for a vehicle or something comparable that does not meet the quality or performance standards that have been set in place. The defective flaws may be so significant that it can affect the safety features and overall value of the vehicle.[1] A lemon can also be an example of a disappointing investment, where an individual expected a certain Return on Investment (ROI). The investment did not even come close to reaching its possible potential. Therefore, it ends up costing more in the end by its poor performance.[2] Occasionally, we experience a relationship in our life that turns out to be a lemon. It can be a friend, a family member, a business partner, or even a significant other. You decide to bring them in as a piece to your life's puzzle, but later find out that they are just not a good fit for you. By their pure existence, they have brought so much confusion to your life that now you must pick up all the pieces of the puzzle and start over. You have invested more than you received in return. These lemons did not make you a better person. They have turned you sour.

Has life ever thrown you a Lemon? Did your Lemon bring a refreshing flavor or a sour aftertaste?

Many times, the lemons in our lives will present themselves as people or things that will later prove to be disappointingly defective. You wanted a certain car that you could not resist. I know it was red, fast, sporty, loaded with all the bells and whistles. You deserve it, right? Maybe you bought a house that was too good to pass on. You now have $100,000 in equity with a three-car garage and six bedrooms. What about the beautiful woman that you could not take your eyes off? 36-24-36, booyah! Oh, and let us not forget the man that could give you all the materialistic things that you have always dreamed of. Yeah, yeah, he is a lawyer. You just could not say no. Here is a word of advice. Never underestimate the power of the Lemon! It will come in a form that makes you weak and brings you to your knees. Only to later be left with the sour aftertaste that takes immeasurable time to dissipate.

All experiences in our lives shape us in some way or another. We all want some sort of explanation of why some turned out good and others not so good. My first marriage, for example, ended in divorce. I used to want answers as to why it happened to my wife and I, but in the end, I have learned to accept that our chapter in each other's story is over. We made mistakes together and separately, as humans do. We both were given the gift of Hope and Courage to face whatever life brings our way. I tell you this because not every experience that ends with disagreements is a Lemon. Sometimes relationships just do not work out, but hopefully you make each other better individuals by the experiences you have together. Embracing the good and bad moments allows us as individuals to grow—whether we see immediate results or not.

Chaos

emons are illusions from reality. They come in disguise, later to be revealed as disappointment, greed, selfishness, brokenness, and most of all . . . a world of chaos. The refreshing taste of Chaos quenches your thirst, which you later find out is only temporary. Her unpredictability keeps you on pins and needles at all times. Your mind is in a constant state of utter confusion as you second guess yourself on a routine basis. You gradually lose clarity, as Chaos instinctively muddies the water. Your daily life is in disarray as she begins to take control. You lose your identity in the mass of disorder. Chaos brings destruction. She rides a high horse in search of power, and hell travels with her. With her deceptive nature, misery is soon to follow.

Some of the relationships that life brings can be particularly challenging. Throw in parenting, bills, schedules, and a job. Now add outcomes such as marriage, more children, divorce, remarriage, blended families, or death. If you live long enough, you most likely have or will encounter at least one of these in your lifetime. I personally have weathered them all. Without being attentive to your surroundings, you will allow these seasonal changes to bring Chaos and havoc with them.

Are you prepared for the change of seasons that life will bring? How will you handle change when it comes unexpectedly?

I was a single dad raising two small children aged five and seven when Chaos walked into my life. Chaos was unpredictably experienced. This was not her first rodeo, as they say. She knew how to present herself in an irresistible chameleon kind of way. The voids that I had could be filled instantly, as she changed to satisfy those needs. It would not take long before I fell victim and got trapped in her web. I could feel myself losing Hope and Courage as Chaos demanded all my time and energy. I was exhausted and tired as I bowed down to her beck and call. Her thoughts came to life by words that flowed from my mouth. She was destroying my life, my business, and my relationships. Chaos brought a disrespectful atmosphere to my world. Her negativity and criticism created a sense of inadequacy. I would cover and make excuses for her rudeness as her words cut like a knife to my family and friends. She was aggressively persuasive in her actions. I left several times but returned for reasons unknown to me at that time. Chaos gave me a mindset of codependency—that I could not live without her. I would try to escape, but the fear of failure and being alone imprisoned me. Our world became complete disorder and confusion. I became concerned as her violent nature rapidly grew. The environment became increasingly dangerous as threats were made to my life. As my fears intensified, we continued to slowly lose our identities. Hope started to lose hope. Courage was no longer courageous. As for me, I was not even close to being Fearless. I felt trapped, with no way out. I had developed the "Why me?" mentality.

So, let us stop and rewind. I would drive around cursing my life while developing the "Why me?" mentality. Then one night it came. I wanted to talk with my dad about the destructive path of Chaos that I was traveling. I could feel his presence telling me that I must take care of Hope and Courage. Then it happened . . . as I slowly opened my eyes, I looked to my left and there stood Hope. I then looked to my right side and I found Courage staring back at me. With words that I will never forget, they said, "Let's go home, Dad, let's go home."

Couples get lost in the maze of confusion and have difficulty finding their way out. I will confess that in more than one of my relationships, this was found to be the case. T.D. Jakes once said, "If they can walk away from you, let them walk. Their part of your story is over."[3] Although I do agree with Jakes, you need to know when to walk away as well.

So, I found myself at the crossroads of life. I knew that my actions would speak louder than any words imaginable . . . . I walked. Never looking back.

Boundaries and Guardrails

Only you can decide when to walk away from the Chaos in your life. Define and choose the direction that you will go. Are you tired of the direction that you are headed?

If the answer is yes, then you have chosen to move forward. Acknowledge that you made a wrong turn, forgive yourself, and learn from it. Once you forgive yourself, then you must forgive others who have wronged you. Furthermore, if you are in a relationship and have hurt one another, you must forgive each other. Internal anger will only cause resistance to positive change. If we are to move forward, then we must truly put the past behind us. We all get off the beaten path from time to time, but no matter what mistakes are made, it is never too late to get back on track.

Have you been holding onto guilt or anger? How has this anger affected your life?

In Cloud and Townsend's book *Boundaries*, it states, "We need to take responsibility for our choices, thereby leading to self-control. We also need to realize that we are in control of our choices, no matter how we feel! I cannot feel your feelings for you. I cannot think for you, nor can I grow for you. Own the fact that you are responsible for yourself. Likewise, I am responsible for myself, my choices, and my actions."[4] Do not get caught up in the blame game. It is always easier to blame someone else rather than taking responsibility.

Second, you must set some parameters for yourself. Learn to say "No" to yourself. This will allow you to say "No" to those difficult decisions that must be made at different seasons of your life. This includes both unhealthy and healthy desires that come your way. Why should we say "No" to certain so-called good things? Plain and simple . . . timing. For instance, you are working at a job that you are extremely happy with. A new firm contacts you to help jump-start their business and offers you a significant pay increase. Although it sounds great and very tempting, you realize a little more work experience is needed before making this leap. You know the money would be immensely helpful. However, your maturity in identifying with your inner self allows you to respectfully say "No." Individual guidelines and knowing your personal identity are both especially important components when developing ownership. Once, these lines are drawn in the sand, you will start to develop a sense of confidence and self-control as to what can cross your defined borders.

Sugar Cubes:

> It is ok to say no. Making excuses or lying only digs holes. Use a good tone and simply decline.

> —B. RHOADS

Dr. Brian D. Rhoads

Sweet Thoughts:

Decide who you want to be with, but don't let
that someone antagonize your own character.

—MATTHEW MCCONAUGHEY

Five

Sweet and Low

The Highs and Lows

I recently went to a well-known restaurant in upstate New York. Our waiter introduced himself as Confusion and kindly asked for our drink order. Naturally, I asked for Sweet Tea. He replied "Sir, I'm sorry but we do not have sweet tea, but I can bring you some sweetener." Going against my gut, I agreed. To my disappointment, our waiter returned with a container filled with "The Pink Stuff." I should have instantly recognized what was going to happen when he said sweetener and better yet, who in the world has a name like Confusion? You see, I cannot blame Confusion for doing his job; he was simply doing his job. He brought exactly what he said he would, "Sweetener." However, what he brought was not pure, it was artificial and even though it appeared sweet, it tasted bitter.

The words "Sweet and Low" sound a lot like life don't they? We are not promised that life will always be sweet and great. In fact, many a time, it brings a lot of lows with it. Remember what I reminded you about the world? It is a tough place and if you are not careful, it will leave you bitter. Life is and can be so sweet. Then one day you wake up and Murphy is sitting right beside you. I guess you are wondering who Murphy is, right? Have you ever heard of Murphy's Law? Murphy states that if anything can go wrong, then it will. What I will say about Murphy is that usually it is not what happens during those low times that matters most. I can almost guarantee you that the lows will come and go. However, the way you respond and handle these low times is what will be life-changing. For the better or worse is up to you.

Misery

We allow circumstances to change our attitude. We allow people to control our moods and behavior. Problems do not have to cause us to lose purpose although we allow them to. You do not have to stay in your wilderness—that wilderness filled with Confusion and lack of direction. If we allow the world to control us, we lose focus and cannot see the forest because of the trees. We cannot see the big picture . . . the real picture—that life is not about us.

Sometimes our identity and image has been distorted so many times that it is beyond recognition. One of my favorite speakers, Steven Furtick, stated, "Disillusionment gets layered upon disappointment, which gets layered upon failure, and our real selves end up buried so far down we don't remember who we actually are."[1]

I see people all the time who wrestle with their identity as to who they really are versus what they want to be in society. For example, Misery is a smart, beautiful, energetic mom. She is bubbly at work, church, Wal-Mart, you name it. Her outward appearance always seems so happy. However, Misery does not receive her name by being authentically happy. Deep down, Misery is empty. Misery wants the perfect selfie for the world to see, to validate her own self-worth, which is ironically laughable in that the root word of "selfie" is "self." Her own self-centeredness has made her develop an agenda. This agenda has given her a sense of entitlement and a belief that money and materialism will fill her void. Misery does not want to be alone and she loves company. Although she only knows what she has been taught, she still is prejudiced by nature and very selective in the physical qualities of the chosen ones, the chosen ones that she and society have placed on a superior pedestal. She will attempt to steal and destroy the lives of those who do not follow her plans. Her relationships fail due to her agenda, where status takes priority over true love. Misery will play the victim if she can gain as much sympathy as possible. She justifies her own actions by pointing out what others did wrong. Misery has lost herself in the piles of distress that she has created in her endless search for the worldly happily ever after.

Deception

On the other hand, I see other people who are conflicted with their identity versus who they want society to think they are. There once was a man that portrayed to the world an image of strong leadership, knowledge, and an enormous sense of spiritual enlightenment. His name was Deception. At first, he was inviting, only to later be considered as unapproachable. He was deceitful in that he portrayed himself as an example for others while, behind closed doors, he acted out in ways men of his status typically do not. He shares the personal thoughts and regretful actions that others had confided in him. He bites the hand that feeds him without any guilt or shame. The respect he desires can be compared to a mirage in the desert, to only disappear as one gets closer with time. His darkest inner secrets filled with deceitfulness haunt him by the second, while the shadows of his confusion consume him. He is lost in the endless search for the key to self-forgiveness. Others will suffer as they have given him all their trust with open hearts and souls. Deception wears a mask of arrogance and holds his cards close to his chest. He is out for himself and personal gain. Sadly enough, Deception is caught in Misery's trap, and only honesty can set them free.

The world has them both as its puppets. They live in fear, as I once did. They play the victim instead of being honest with themselves and those around them. We cannot be committed to a worldly system more than the heavenly source—the source that created it all. Once we start taking responsibility for our own actions and are truly desperate for a clean heart then the real change will start to happen. Desperation is the door that breakthrough walks through. You are your best when you are authentic to your core!

Has Confusion ever brought artificial sweetness into your life to only bring low times and Misery with it? Often, we get so caught up in the world that we begin to believe that our own Misery is our happiness. But like "The Pink Stuff," Misery is NOT real and is not pure. It is deceitful in its birth and it loves company. Our Misery begins to be all that we know because it is comfortable and familiar. Sometimes we are attracted to the same type of people and stay stuck in our own Misery. We are afraid to change due to the honest fact that we are creatures of habit. You do the same things that you have always done, date the same type of person that you have always been with, react the same way that you always react, expecting the result to be different. You have conditioned your mind to believe that your Misery is your happiness.

Now I am not at all an art gallery type of guy, but have you ever seen the movie *Clueless*? There is a scene where Tai ask her friend Cher "Do you think that she is pretty?" Cher replies, "NO, she is a full-on Monet." Tai says, "What's a Monet?" Cher says, "It's a painting see; from far away, it's ok but up close, it's a big ole mess."[2]

This is a lot like the Misery in our own lives. So many times, when we choose a person to be in our lives, we strictly choose the superficial attributes that our society has made important. However, once you get up close and get to know them, you begin to realize that they are a complete mess. In the process, you realize that the misery that they bring into your life is unhealthy. But you convince yourself that your Misery is your happiness. This realization gives you a familiar knot in the pit of your stomach, which has been ignored for some time now—your gut.

Listen to Your Gut

Remember when Confusion told me he would bring me some sweetener and I agreed. My gut knew it did not feel right but

I did it anyway. Looking back, red flags were present when Misery entered my life. It felt comfortable and looked familiar to what I had grown accustomed to with past experiences. Misery was similar to Chaos, only in a younger less-experienced version. Blinded by her youth and charm, I ignored the warning signs.

God places warning signs around us to keep us from making some of the decisions that we make. But we arrogantly ignore these signs and silence our gut to only do what we want to do anyway. We have the audacity to think that we can handle life on our own, only to then ask God to fix the problems that we have created after we mess up. As humans, we have been given the ability to make decisions based on logic and emotion. Gut provides you with the unique ability to decide instinctively and without reason. Gut is that feeling in your stomach that gives an unexplainable sense of "I just know." Which is humorously contradictory because if you "just knew," then why did you do it? I genuinely believe that gut comes from the wisdom and clarity that we have gained from our past, personal life experiences, or experiences that others share with us. I once heard the saying, "If you're going to go through it then you might as well grow through it." Well, it is true. Your personal gut does not always have the distinction of keeping you from making bad decisions. Your gut is also protective in its nature and it can strongly pull you in a direction that causes you to listen to your mind and body. For example, if your body is telling you that something physically does not feel right, then you should certainly listen. Your gut can also allow you to have compassion and sympathy for others. It helps us to gain peace of mind that the money we give a hungry homeless person will be used for food and not alcohol. Think about your gut as being that innermost feeling that helps you slow down and find the Wisdom needed to make a clear, conscious mature decision. So again, do not confuse that pit in your stomach as a sign of anxiety or worry. Instead, think of it as your ally when those battles arise.

Anxiety

I grew up surrounded by a free-spirited and carefree soul that lived by her own rules. She was a rebel and lived life to the fullest. Her life could not have better been described than by Lesley Gore's song "You Don't Own Me." Whenever she wanted to go, she went. When something was on her mind, she let it be known. Several years later, a sense of uneasiness began to evolve with the premature birth of her daughter, Innocence. With the physical health problems that developed, Anxiety began to take shape within this free-spirited soul. Her mindset of constant worry only strengthened as her questions had no answers.

Anxiety brings feelings of worry with her. Her uneasiness is constant in stressful situations. She becomes agitated when left in suspense. Her apprehensiveness and fears keep her from progress. Anxiety does not exist for unknown reasons and believes these circumstances justify her agitation. She over thinks, which makes her nervous about taking chances. Anxiety anticipates the worst outcome in any event. She requires much clarity in decision-making and without it, confusion takes hold.

Does everything in your life seem fuzzy right now? Quite frankly, you might feel like you do not have a clue as to what your next move is going to be. To be honest, it is scary and can give you an unhealthy sense of anxiety. PsychologyToday.com states, "There are several differences between worry and anxiety. While we tend to experience worry in our heads, anxiety affects the entire body. Worry is more specifically problem focused which leads to a more diffuse sense of anxiousness. Therefore, worry can and will lead to inevitable problem solving. While when anxious, our minds wander without any solutions."[3]

When Anxiety and I were younger, we would spend a week at our grandparents' house during summer vacation. On several occasions, we would eagerly wait on the porch for our grandfather to come home from a hard day of work. One night after arriving, he slowly got out of his old blue and white truck (Chevy, of course) and walked toward the porch. After walking up the two steps, he moved his hand toward a bush planted by the front screened door. Grabbing a branch, he closed his eyes as he slowly rubbed a leaf between his fingertips and then immediately entered the house. The following day, we noticed the same routine. Out of curiosity, we decided to ask Grandpa the significance of the tree.

"Grandpa, why do you rub that bush every day when you come home?" Anxiety asked.

He slowly smiled and said, "I planted this bush when I thought about a story I heard years ago about a similar tree. Each day, this man came home from a long hard day. His job was stressful and with that came lots of problems. However, every day before entering the house he would rub this one tree in the front yard. The man made a pact with himself to not bring his problems home with him. So, before walking in to see his wife and children, he rubbed the tree, leaving his troubles there with it."

reached. As he choked down his breakfast, a loud thunderous sound erupted as the boat violently shook. With alarms now sounding, he rapidly rushed outside to a world of total destructive pandemonium and disbelief. Fire, debris, and wounded lay all over. They had been hit by one of two torpedoes sent by the enemy German submarine U-486. The *Leopoldville* was damaged badly and slowly sinking! The wounded ship was five miles from the coast and would not be able to complete her journey. While assessing the damage, it was soon discovered that the explosion had destroyed many of the lifeboats. Furthermore, many others had been lost at sea during the commotion. The number of lifeboats needed to remove the survivors was not enough. It was quickly determined that a new exit strategy would need to be made in order to survive. The *Leopoldville* continued to radio and flash for help with little success. Many allied forces failed to acknowledge the call for help as many of the crewman were ashore celebrating the holiday. Meanwhile, my grandfather prepared himself mentally and physically as he watched his fellow crewmen jump from the sinking ship. Life jackets were issued to each soldier, but the instructions were not understood as they were in Flemish. As sailors jumped from a height forty-fifty feet, many snapped their necks as the collars of their life jackets were not manually held down upon impact in the water. Others jumped in fear with their helmets strapped on tightly. They too made a costly mistake of not releasing the chinstrap, causing their necks to break as they hit the concrete-like waves of the water. With little time to waste, my grandfather carefully put on his life vest and found his pocketknife tucked away in his pants. He knew that his knife would be needed to make himself some type of raft once he hit the frigid waters. He would not make the same mistake that his fellow sailors had made. The ship was rapidly sinking by the minute and he knew that he must jump. He carefully released the chin strap from his helmet and held down the collar on his life vest. As he placed one leg after the other over the ship's rail, he found himself looking down into the debris and the oil-filled ocean. With one swift jump, he plunged below. The water was freezing and took his breath away as he sank beneath the surface. He quickly removed his pocketknife, cutting rope, ship debris, and anything he could find to make a floating device for himself and others.

It took over an hour before it was learned that the *Leopoldville* was sinking. Allied vessels might have served for rescue, but all had cold engines and lack of crew members attending Christmas gatherings. Forces in Cherbourg failed to mobilize a rescue party before the *Leopoldville* sank later that night. Once the rescue parties reached the scene, Grandpa knew he was one of the lucky ones. Through his courage and preparation, he was able to survive this moment of crisis. Most of the men pulled from the water had already frozen to death on that unforgettable Christmas Eve. Seven hundred and sixty-three American soldiers were killed that night and the bodies of four hundred and ninety-three were never recovered from the freezing waters.[4]

Do you believe in coincidence? Better yet, do you believe in coincidental fate?

Out of all the books that my son Hope could have chosen from the library coincidentally, he was led to the *Leopoldville*. As far as that infamous pocketknife that saved my grandfather's life is concerned, ironically it has been in my possession for the last several years. Before my grandfather passed away, he gave it to my father. Years later, my father passed it on to me. One more comparable fact to ponder. On December 24, 1944, my grandfather's world was shaken with tremendous thunder as he would escape death. On December 24, 2011, my world too came to a halt as time momentarily stood still . . . my father died. Sixty-seven years to the date! Coincidental fate? You be the judge.

How have you prepared for any crisis that will come your way?

Prepare for the unexpected. My grandfather was destined for greatness, which came through his conscious decision, commitment, and will to survive. Just like the *Leopoldville*, life will have its own battles. I can almost guarantee that at some point you will be attacked unexpectedly. You most likely will face difficulties related to family, friends, work, health, or finances.

Crisis Management

For example, have your ever experienced a life-changing crisis or life-battling circumstances? You just got laid off from your job and you do not know where your next meal will come from. Maybe your spouse does not love you anymore and wants a divorce. Or your doctor just informed you that you have cancer. Do you want to survive? Then you must fight. As the character Rocky Balboa once said, "It ain't about how hard you hit, it's about how hard you can get hit and keep moving forward."[5] Before Grandpa climbed over the rails to jump, he knew that he must take care of himself first. If you do not take care of yourself, who will? He assessed the situation to make a conscious healthy decision. You will be of little help to anyone if you are not healthy or don't have a strong mindset. Just as Grandpa plunged into the waters, you too might just have to take a leap of faith.

Without preparing a crisis management plan, you risk the possibility of bringing unnecessary negative energy into your life—problems such as depression, anger, resentment, and feelings of failure. Do not let negative words lead to negative thoughts. Instead, use positive actions and reinforcement words to fight your way to victory. The life vest, the helmet, and even the pocket knife were all tools that assisted in the survival of many soldiers. However, without proper instruction and preparedness, these survival tools proved to be useless for some. Countless times, we are given clues and possession of the tools needed to get out of battles. Tools such as morality, ethics, personal gut, and clear wisdom. However, we fail to recognize and ignore these signals. We are not forced to do anything, but if we follow instructions and suggestions, positive results are more likely to develop.

Set goals for yourself. Focus on your strengths not your weaknesses. Lean on friends and family. Big dreams require great teams recognizing different strengths. When you combine what two can do, it exponentially increases. Realize that you are unstoppable. Grasp the concept that life is 10 percent what happens to you and 90 percent how you respond.

Sugar Cubes:

Ships do not sink from water that is on the outside. . . ships sink because of the water that gets inside. Do not allow yourself to sink by what is happening around. Stay afloat!

Sweet Thoughts:

_____

_____

_____

_____

_____

_____

_____

_____

_____

_____

_____

_____

_____

_____

_____

_____

_____

_____

_____

_____

_____

_____

_____

_____

_____

_____

Good timber does not grow with ease, the
stronger the winds, the stronger the trees.

—UNKNOWN

Six

ADDING SPLENDA TO YOUR LIFE

I used to hunt occasionally with my grandfather when I was a kid.

He would tell me, "Sit very quietly and as still as possible."

Do you know how hard it is to sit still as a ten-year-old? So, I asked him, "Why Grandpa?" His reply was priceless.

Grandpa replied, "Because if you can see it, then it can see you. If you sit back and listen, it will eventually show itself."

Wow! Think about that one.

I remembered this later in my adult life one afternoon, when I was fortunate enough to hunt at a members' only hunting club, Cow Island, where the deer are plentiful and huge. As I sat in the cold, it came a "Gulley Washer" as my grandpa would say. It rained and rained for two hours straight. I may never get to hunt here again I thought, so I decided to tough it out. Then, suddenly, it stopped almost instantly. Just like Grandpa said, I reminded myself to not get sloppy now, but simply sit back and listen. It was so quiet as the raindrops fell from the trees. Then it happened just like he said it would. A massive twelve-point deer and I were staring right at each other. It seemed like an eternity, as neither of us would even blink.

Suddenly, the gigantic buck started walking toward me gracefully and quietly with a continual stare. When he finally reached me, something came over me as I continued to listen. I could hear Grandpa's voice very clearly. "If you can see it, then it can see you." At that moment, it seemed as though time stood still, and I did the unexpected. I let him walk. It is difficult to explain in words the experience that we shared together, but it was special. Even though we did not speak the same language, I believe, from our encounter, that we both learned to have the deepest respect for one another.

Sometimes, sitting back and being quiet and patient while listening will give you the wisdom and clarity in making the decision that is best for you at that moment. I am not at all saying that you should agree with Misery, Deception, and Chaos. What I am saying, however, is that you should acknowledge that they are real because without their existence you would not have gained the wisdom and strength to prepare you to get through the next struggle. Keep in mind that difficulty does not and is not meant to get you off track but, along with perseverance, can allow for personal development.

Wisdom

Wisdom is bold and stands tall in his thinking. He is knowledgeable and provides good judgment. His experience brings foresight to the inevitable that will come. This experience allows you to not make the same mistakes that he made. Wisdom is ethical and moral. His calmness gives him a supernatural ability in making impossible solutions a reality. He is not prejudiced and does not take sides. Wisdom is unbiased and calls it like it is. Wisdom provides protection when he is called upon. He brings discernment in the outcome of situations. Wisdom is compassionate, but stern when need be. He is the game changer when one feels lost. He does not sweat under pressure for he is confident in what he brings to the table. Wisdom is both the alpha and omega of integrity and character. Wisdom brings personal growth, providing Clarity with decision-making when your back is against the wall.

Clarity

When Clarity teams with Wisdom, one starts to develop a new perception of their surroundings and conditions. Clarity brings a total sense of clearness and understanding because she has been here before. She can see the character and intentions of people from afar. Clarity is truthful and direct. She calls "a spade a spade", referring to it is what it is. Clarity is consistent and transparent in her nature. She provides explanations for moral reasoning and logic. Clarity provides good direction and is your compass when storms develop. The clouds do not block her vision as she knows the light is coming soon.

The Lightning Tree

With storms and clouds, sometimes comes lightning. This reminds me of a story about an old tree that sat in the middle of the little town square. The tree was just a normal old tree, nothing special. However, over the years, it had gradually become a famous attraction called the Lightning Tree. The tree had been struck by lightning several times over the years, but still somehow managed to survive the damaging blows that came with the storms. The tree became incredibly significant for the community as a symbol of its survival. As time progressed, people started to notice the leaves changing from green to brown as the tree appeared to be slowly dying. There was a consensus that the lightning had finally taken its toll on the famous old tree. You see, when lightning hits a tree, the electricity sometimes travels down the trunk to the root structure. Many times, the tree will appear healthy on the outside, but the internal damage will not show itself until a later time. This progressive internal deterioration can cause the weakened tree to slowly decline and eventually die.

One day, a man passing through noticed some bugs at the base of the tree. They appeared to have been there for a surprisingly good while, but apparently had gone unnoticed. As he inspected further, he realized that they were bark beetles.

Why does this matter? Why is it relevant to the story? Bear with me.

Bark beetles primarily go after weakened stressed trees. They tunnel their way through the outer damaged bark to get to the healthy underlying layer. Because these trees are figuratively speaking tired, they simply do not have the motivation and energy to fight off the beetles. Therefore, the beetles end up killing the tree by cutting off transportation of water and nutrients.[1]

Here is the point. The old tree obviously took some major damaging blows during its lifetime. It survived those numerous hits time after time. Although it appeared to be healthy on the outside, no one really knew the true internal damage and scars that had developed in the old tree. People used obvious reasoning in that maybe the lightning was just too much of a punch for the well-known attraction. What they failed to realize and ignored was that the little insignificant beetles were actually what was killing the tree.

As humans, we all experience major significant hits in our lives. It is inevitable; they will come and go. There is no doubt that the big punches sting, but never undermine the importance of the unnoticed little hits that throw the final swing and can knock a person out.

Little Things Matter

Sometimes you have just had enough. These so-called little unimportant pebbles are just building up into bigger and bigger mountains by the minute. You feel like you are being buried by the mounds of stress that have developed. Deep down you realize that those pebbles or words are indeed incredibly significant to you personally. You have lost countless hours, days, and possibly years of wishful thinking to never hear the important words that emotionally matter.

You feel unappreciated by no one saying a simple "Thank you."
You feel unloved without a heartfelt . . . "I Love You."
You work hard . . . never to hear "Good job."

You did your best, wishing for the words . . ."I'm proud of you."

People who say that the little words of affirmation do not matter are the very ones who need to hear those words as well. Bigger, visual materialistic items such as large expensive gifts are commonly more identified and valued by society. When life brings unbalanced seasons, your personal priority list seems to change as well. With this change, consistently focusing your attention on important words and phrases will provide a level of respect and love to those that are significant in your life. In return, you will be amazed at the reciprocation that will follow.

Consistency

Consistency means being present in the moment and not disengaged. Being consistently there when needed, not constantly absent when conditions are unfavorable. When one is consistent, momentum builds. This momentum brings a favorable routine and a positive attitude.—an attitude of what you see is what you get. His views are held firmly together, and he is not swayed easily by other outside influences. Consistency leads to improvement and believes that practice makes perfect. His repetitive patterns bring trust that optimistic results will follow.

Be cautiously aware of the weeds that will occasionally develop in the root of your life. By diligent pruning, you can prevent these tiny multiplying nuisances from choking out your happiness. Consistency combines with motivation in creating a self-disciplined attitude. If you want to be a great father, then you must be dependably present and active. If you want to be a great spouse, then you must be steady in your pruning and in watering the areas that you want to grow. This is an everyday process and requires motivation. It is necessary to identify your own flaws, which leads to the development of self-motivation and the desire to be the best version of yourself.

Sugar Cubes:

> Never get tired of doing the little things
> for others. Sometimes those little things
> occupy the biggest part of their hearts.

—UNKNOWN

Sweet Thoughts:

_____

_____

_____

_____

_____

_____

_____

_____

_____

_____

_____

_____

_____

_____

_____

_____

_____

_____

_____

_____

_____

_____

_____

_____

_____

_____

_____

_____

And then it happens . . . . One day you wake up
and you are in this place. You are in this place
where everything feels right. Your heart is calm.
Your soul is on fire. Your thoughts are positive.
Your vision is clear. You're at peace with where
you've been, at peace with what you've been
through and at peace where you're headed.

—THE MIND'S JOURNAL

Seven

EQUAL

As I walked down the hall, two women caught my eye; they were talking casually in a nearby conference room. One of the women I knew, the other I did not. What I did know was that they both were highly educated. One of the women was very outspoken and had an animated personality. She used her hands a lot when she talked and laughed as she spoke. The other woman was younger, attractive, and highly intelligent. She carried a sense of peace with her. Peace was very engaged in the conversation but did not have time to get in a word. She laughed as the other woman continued to talk. Although she was very engaged, I felt as though she was trapped and needed an out.

I said, "Hey, do you guys have one of those fortune cookies for me?"

The younger woman quickly replied, "Maybe, who is asking?" and gently threw one to me. The conversation stopped, and we all went our own direction.

The next experience that I am about to share with you is about one of the most eye-opening events of my life.

As I continued down the hall, an older gentleman named Prejudice said, "Hey bud, can I talk to you for a second?"

I slowly walked in his office, and I said, "Sure."

Prejudice stated, "I couldn't help but notice that you were talking to Peace a moment ago".

I could feel my eyebrows begin to curl; I said, "Yes, you did."

"Well, you know she is Black! There are certain people that would not agree."

I had to process this comment quickly. What was Prejudice saying to me? Was it a threat? Did he think I was blind? Who would not agree? I knew good and well what color she was. I did not care who agreed. I felt attacked. At that moment, I realized that the old southern plantation mentality still existed and was staring me right in the face.

With a smirk, I bluntly replied," Black? When did this happen? She is Black?"

With his eyes now widened and his head cocked back, he simply said, "Watch yourself."

You see, I purposely did not tell you the color of the two women talking because up until this point it did not matter. Did it? Both are intelligent, articulate, sophisticated women equal in their jobs and titles. We all went in our own directions, as I stated. But what direction is that? I, like a lot of you, had become embarrassingly numb to the reality that racism still exists. This opened my eyes to what was really going on around me. I have always had many friends of different races. However, I have not ever put myself in their shoes until this day.

Prejudice could not get past the fact that this woman was equal to him in all respects in terms of what she had accomplished. Peace did not have a choice regarding the color of her skin. In all fairness, Prejudice did not have a choice either. Where Prejudice does have a choice is in deciding which direction he will go. However, the direction that he normally chooses allows him to live in absolute hatred for so long that it becomes a normal way of life. When dealing with Prejudice, remember that we are dealing with illogical creatures motivated by their own insecurities and society's approval of status and appearance. Prejudice has no boundaries. It will hate because of the existence of its counterparts of Deception, Misery, and Chaos. Only when we individually decide to alter these controlling factors in our lives will we begin to genuinely enjoy the Peace that is waiting on us.

Sugar Cubes:

> No one is born hating another person because of
> the color of his skin, or his background, or his
> religion. People must learn to hate, and if they
> can learn to hate, they can be taught to love.

—Nelson Mandela

Have you ever judged a book by its cover and later realized that your convictions were biased?

Color Blindness

Color blindness usually involves the inability to see reds and greens. I have often wondered what would happen if we possessed the inability to see shades of whites and blacks. Although every one of us should be valued and appreciated for the pigmentation of our skin . . . what if we were all color blind? Without the negative stereotypes that are derived from an individual's phenotypical characteristics, would racism exist today without the existence of colorism?

While reading this book, have you thought about how all these sweetener packets are different colors? Pure sugar is white, Sweet and Low is pink, Splenda is yellow, and Equal is blue. Ironically, these packets are all different colors yet sweet in their own way. The use of color has such power in influencing communication and reactions amongst each of us. Through our blindness and without even realizing it, we see the colors of our surrounding objects as the norm. Trees are green, the sky is blue . . . the list could go on and on. While our minds are conditioned and blind to these colors, we accept these visual characteristics of any object as fact. Except when it comes to people. Mindboggling! We develop an "all of a sudden" awareness and 20/20 vision that a person looks different from us. Therefore, they MUST be different from us. Not by the color of their hair, not by the color of their eyes, but by the color of their skin. Why is that?

All these sweeteners bring their own unique characteristic flavor. However, the artificial sweeteners are hundreds of times sweeter than pure sugar. In fact, Equal is more than two hundred times sweeter than sugar. Think about if equality could make the world two hundred times sweeter than it currently is.[1] The color blinded accomplishments and results that would transpire simply by putting our unbiased, nonracial sweet gifts and talents together in making this altered artificial place better. Perhaps then we would open our minds to the pure sweetness that could exist like we have never seen before.

Recognizing Peace

Why does it storm? To appreciate the rain. Then why does it rain, I might ask? To appreciate the sunshine. We all tend to lose focus and forget to appreciate the good in our lives from time to time. It is perfectly normal. I believe that these are trials and tests that God has given us to bring us back to reality and closer to him. Trials can be exceedingly difficult events or seasons in our lives, while tests are specific challenges that reveal strength and maturity. Tests come to prove, reveal, and strengthen. Therefore, going through these Chaotic and Misery chapters are necessary to finding inner Peace. Never waste your pain. Use your experiences to help others in getting through the tough times that life brings.

How do you recognize Peace? How did I identify with Peace?

You must define what it means to you personally. Peace brings friendship and understanding. Peace is comfortable and brings no stress. She is nonjudgmental and very practical in her thinking. She is calming when situations become tense. Peace teams with Wisdom, Hope, and Courage into providing Clarity that you are going in the right Direction. Peace brings happiness and allows you to be yourself. Peace accepts your flaws and weaknesses with your strengths. She brings loyalty and will fight by your side. Peace brings respect but asks for the same in return. Peace only brings love and will lay down her life for you if you will do the same. Having Peace and being Fearless gives strength in building Faith that no challenge is too big. Peace is the calm before the storm and the silence after battles of good reason.

Fearful Finds Peace

Peace intrigued me. I loved the friendship and calmness that came with her. I was able to be myself. However, it was uncomfortable at the same time, which led to several questions. Questions like what is everyone going to think of me? Do I choose the superficial artificial qualities that I always have or follow the Peace that I now feel? The Peace that I prayed for felt so natural, but I still pushed her away. I was Fearful! I cared way too much what everyone thought! I was guilty of putting thought bubbles in people's heads when in reality no one probably even cared. I was weak, egotistical, and self-centered. With that, I left the door open and Misery rushed in.

Sometimes your greatest Wisdom comes after your biggest mistake.

Let us get this straight. Your Misery is unique and quite different from everyone else's. It is your own Misery. It can be a person, a job, a habit . . . ANYTHING. Furthermore, it can change at any given time to something else. Misery will demand change, and change may very much be needed in your life. But I will say, do not ever change anything about yourself for someone else. The real transformation to change can only occur when one finally accepts that they need to change and acts by wanting to change.

Misery knew my weakness, as it does for all of us. Others see it, but you are somehow blinded by your own selfish desires. I began to live a double life—one with Peace, the other in Misery. Misery brought instant gratification with a combination of Chaos and Deception. My life became a ticking time bomb filled with lies, lust, deceitfulness, and self-centeredness. I made promises to Misery I could not or did not want to keep. Meanwhile, Peace was peace. She continued to be the calmness that my life needed. However, with Peace comes Wisdom and Clarity. When Misery exists, Peace tends to disappear for periods in our lives. They cannot coexist.

When Peace found out that Misery existed in my life, she questioned why and wanted answers.

Eyebrows curled, Peace simply asked me, "What can Misery give you that I can't? You are doing the very things that you stated you do not want."

Hesitantly, I stated, "Nothing . . . I don't know."

Peace looked me in the eyes and paused for a moment before she replied, "I do." Then, she simply placed her arm against mine and said nothing.

Silence! The pure silence that causes your mouth to dry, palms to sweat, and your stomach to roll. The silence that comes when truth exposes you.

At that moment, I had become a part of the very categorical characteristic that I had always tried to remove myself from . . . discrimination. My reality check had been delivered. I never considered myself discriminatory, just preferential. The characteristics of dark brown hair, brown eyes, and traditional white-skinned American had always been my preference and habitual choosing. Wait a minute; did I just say white skin? If it had never really mattered to me, then why was I so afraid of Peace?

My integrity and character, the very core that I had always tried to protect, had been compromised . . . all in a few seconds.

I could not help but think about my dad talking so passionately about character while protecting the family name. In his soft raspy voice, he would say, "If you lose some money, you lose nothing. If you lose your health you lose something, but if you lose your character, you lose everything."

So, Fearful as I was, I took the most familiar path that I was conditioned to by society's standards and I ran. I ran as fast as I could from the Peace that my heart so desperately desired to the Misery filled life that I felt society wanted for me. I was ashamed of who I had become. As several months passed, the guilt and shame started to take its toll. On one Sunday morning, it hit me like a ton of bricks. I heard a message from one of my favorite speakers, John Siebling.

"When the pain to stay the same becomes greater than the pain it takes to change, then we become willing to change."[2]

I was tired emotionally, mentally, and spiritually. I was ready to change. I was numb and did not feel life. I could not take it anymore and I decided to come clean with my own inner struggles. Wisdom and Clarity pointed to honesty as being the only way.

Later in the week, I sat down with my Misery and told her the Peace that I had found in my life. I told her when I found Peace, how I found Peace, and how she made me feel. The feeling that I had from having a clear, clean conscience was refreshing and exhilarating. For the first time in my life, I felt free in that moment.

When you recognize and attempt to remove the Misery in your life, be prepared. Remember what I said earlier, Misery does not like to be alone. She will not go away with ease from your life. She would continue to control my mindset and convince me to make her a priority in my life. Once the race of Peace was revealed, Misery, in response, showed her own true colors.

"They are different from us," she would say. "Their hair is different, that is gross!" "My mom would kill me if I ever dated one!"

At that instance, Misery gave birth to her new full name— Misery Deception Prejudice. Again, I had realized at that very moment that in our world prejudice still exists. If I continued to live a life with Misery and Deception in it, then I would be compromising everything that had I always stood for. With this realization, I found who I was and changed the game.

Accepting Your Peace

The wisdom that I have gained through my experiences directed me towards my Faith. I was at my last resort, which should have been my first. I leaned into God and began to humbly pray. I started praying and asking for specifics, but not in a selfish manner. A sense of Peace began to come over me again. She had been right in front of me all along. I then realized that some of life's greatest opportunities are not always that obvious.

I had prayed for a Christian woman who could build me up and support me as a Christian man. Someone who would love my children and family. Someone who did not have ulterior motives with an agenda. I even began to pray for specifics to blend with the timing of my life changes. I prayed for a woman who had never been married, a woman who did not have children, who was not from my area, who had my same educational standards, and a comparable stable career; most importantly, someone who was equally yoked. I have learned in life that if you do not ask, you will never know. Humorously, I could sense God lovingly and laughing looking down on me. Here is the punch line. God gave me EXACTLY what I had prayed for in Peace. My time had finally arrived, as only he knew that I was ready. In those prayers, not one time was race ever brought up.

Race is bigger than our own individuality. There is no one race superior to the other. Our own individuality will only be of significance when we can learn to see all races as equal in our own eyes.

Being Fearless

Your transformation from Fearful to Fearless will not come easily. Once Peace is part of your life, Misery will team with Chaos and Deception to try to destroy the harmony that now exists in your world. The ruthless win-or-lose nature that battles bring can sometimes lead to more short- and long-term wars. Unfortunately, Misery, Deception, and Chaos have their own agendas, which involve failure and doubt.

How did I become Fearless? Initially, I had to get over myself. Accept that I am no better than anyone. I was not nearly as important as I thought I was. Sure, people watch you and me and our actions. For what? To simply justify their own actions. So, once I took myself off the pedestal that I had placed myself on, the clarity of what was important in my life started to clearly show.

Being Fearless requires much determination. So, I say it again—the Fearless will stand up for what he believes. The Fearless are not afraid to go against society's mindset—that what society thinks matters most. Fearless is prepared for battles such as race and prejudice that come his way. The Fearless looks you in the eyes and says, "Give me your best shot." He is humble in accepting his weaknesses and failures; they only make him stronger. Being Fearless sometimes requires silence which in return brings inner Peace, Wisdom, and Clarity. Fearless owns his mistakes and is not afraid to say, "I'm sorry." He believes when others do not. The Fearless say yes when haters say no. Fearless loves when others hate. He picks the battles that matter most. Being Fearless means taking chances and not looking back. Being Fearless means standing out in a crowd. He knows how to talk the talk and walk the walk. Fearless is being open to new ideas. He will speak up and is not afraid of change. With this, Fearless realizes that whatever he does right now will echo an eternity.

Being a Zoology major, I was taught endlessly about habitat and adaptation. While ecosystems and environments are natural, these elements constantly change over time. This requires an adaptation of the organisms and creatures to their new environments. It becomes necessary for the animals to transform and alter their behavior to survive. For example, many camouflage and blend with their surroundings, which protects them against the predators or enemies that come their way.[3]

People in correlation are remarkably similar to this theory. Some simply do not change at all and symbolically die through their unacceptance of the adaptation process. On the other side, the strong evolve and change completely, thus changing their own habitat through the transformation. They make their world stronger by their pure existence, which in turn makes others around them stronger as well. They naturally work together with an instinctive will to change. A Fearless mindset involves adaptation in an ever-changing environment. This adaptation involves a desire to evolve into something new through true change.

Sugar Cubes:

Inner peace begins the moment you choose not to live in fear by allowing another person or event to control your emotions.

Judgmentalism

Judgmentalism involves an environment consumed with Misery and Chaos. It will soon give birth to character flaws such as hypocrisy, selfishness, destruction, and gossip. Unfortunately, when one is considered judgmental, it is usually of a negative nature. Judgment involves rushing into opinions about someone or something without good reason. Typically, these opinions are cruel and unfair.

Judgmental condemns someone as being unworthy and not good as themselves in comparison. "There is a big difference between making judgments and being judgmental. Making judgments comes from a balanced and neutral mind. On the other hand, judgmentalism comes from an imbalanced and reactive mind that is seeking to protect itself from being hurt by others."[4] In an environment that is consumed with Misery and Chaos, other negative character flaws present themselves.

I recently had a discussion with one of my colleagues about general adaptation. Think about the irony of how organisms and living creatures around us naturally and instinctively adapt to their environments. In contrast, humans are unwilling to shift their actions and ways of thinking in a world that is drastically changing. Why? The answer is noticeably clear. The lack of an instinctive will to change. We are taught and conditioned from our environment as to what we believe and how we live. How you were raised. Where you grew up and currently live. The people you work and associate with daily. All these factors can drastically influence human choices. So, yes, we, like the other creatures around us, have three basic choices. One, we can do nothing. Stay exactly where you are and do absolutely nothing. Two, you can decide to blend with the world. This is what most people will choose as it gives them a sense of protection and security of acceptance. Three, you can decide to evolve and change. This fearless change includes involving yourself in the process of changing your surroundings and the ways of thinking that exists.

This discussion led to our next scenario. You have become extremely sick and have been through all treatments possible. Your last resort for survival is a heart transplant. If you do not receive this new heart, you have been told that you will indeed die. Coincidentally, there is a donor available, but not of your ethnicity or race. Do you choose to receive their heart or refuse out of pure hatred and prejudice? Let us put a twist on it. What if it was not you that was sick? It was your significant other or best friend . . . or better yet, your child. What is your answer?

Pause for a second as you think about this.

Go into your bathroom and look in the mirror. Who do you see? Do you like who you see? Mirrors do not lie. Constant self-assessment will push and motivate you to keep yourself in check, thereby creating a true inner reflection. Let your mirror be your teacher. We only see what we want to see in our reflections. However, do not forget that we are also mirrors to others. May our beliefs and actions be the reflections that others will desire and grow from.

Sugar Cubes:

> Be more concerned with your character than
> your reputation. Character is what you really are.
> Reputation is what people say you are. Reputation
> is often based on character-but not always.
>
> —JOHN WOODEN

Sweet Thoughts:

Eight

Formula to the Sweet Life

$$\frac{\text{(Hope + Courage) Belief}}{\text{(Clarity + Wisdom) Direction}} = \text{Fearless Faith}$$

As I drove through the parking lot to my backdoor, I put my truck in park to gather my things. I quickly turned my head as I suddenly heard a pecking noise on my driver's side window. To my surprise, a beautiful red cardinal was perched on my window seal, staring back at me. After making eye contact for what seemed like an eternity, it gently flew to the nearby fence. With one last gaze into my eyes, it softly disappeared into the Eve of the New Year. The following morning, I decided to sleep in a little to catch up on some long-needed rest. Coincidentally, I found myself in a dream filled with a forest full of trees and countless red cardinals.

The birds were deep crimson and flew gracefully from tree to tree. The wind was swift as it whistled through the leaves. Clouds moved quickly across the bright blue background. Then it happened . . . a cardinal flew into my hand, stared me in the eyes, and I woke up.

I really did not think much of all of this until the peace within me became curious about the symbolism or possible meaning of the birds. What I found was astonishing. Red cardinals have been considered by many to be spiritual messengers. "A cardinal can be representative of a loved one who has passed. It has been said that when you see one, they are visiting you or guarding you from something. They seem to make unique appearances during times of celebration such as a New Year to let you know that they are always with you. They remind us to stay focused in achieving our goals. They symbolize self-confidence and strength in one's abilities."[1] As far as the cardinal's crimson color goes, it is symbolic of faith—reminding us to stay strong and fight through circumstances that might look bleak.

Some cultures believe that cardinals help them predict the seasons and which direction to go or travel. This sense of direction is customarily in a positive forward manner. No matter the story or belief, there seems to be meaning to the signs that are in our paths, which we ignore all the time.[2]

It is no accident that the word "cardinal" comes from the Latin word "cardo" which means "hinge or axis". Imagine this hinge as being like one that would be on a door.[3] A doorway that is open for change if we would only take it. A change for the world that is filled with hope and courage by believing and wanting to experience real transformation. A change that gives us clear vision and wisdom in knowing that we are going in a forward direction. A direction that allows your fearless faith to exponentially increase by bringing peace to your life. A Peace where we have nothing to lose, but everything to gain.

. . . A sweeter life!

Sugar Cubes: Formula to the Sweet Life

$$\frac{(H+C)B}{(C+W)D} = F^2$$

What is your formula to becoming a Fearless Faithful person? Only you know. When will you begin?

One day or day one? You decide . . . .

Dear Peace,

When I first met you, I never imagined that we would become what we are. As confusing to me as it all was, along with our presence came friendship and intellectual understanding . . . an understanding of my world that no one has ever been able to grasp. You brought happiness and allowed me to be myself. You teamed with Hope, Courage, and Clarity in keeping me going in the only sensible direction—forward. You accepted my flaws and weaknesses followed by underserving forgiveness. Through all the miserable chaos, you continuously provided loyalty and respect to me. From the moment that I stopped running, I knew one truth was real . . . I fell in love with you. A love so deep that it includes my mind, heart, and soul. I now know that by persevering through all the challenges and hurts, you were my reward. It all had to happen for you to happen. In return, I give you my heart . . . a heart that brings immeasurable love, faithful support, and unconditional protection. I can never thank you enough for the true internal peace that you brought to my life. Because of you, I have become Fearless.

Always,

Fearless

Sweet Thoughts:

_____

_____

_____

_____

_____

_____

_____

_____

_____

_____

_____

_____

_____

_____

_____

_____

_____

_____

_____

_____

_____

_____

_____

_____

_____

_____

_____

Notes

Introduction

1. "T.D. Jakes—Nothing Just Happens," YouTube video, 2:21 posted by Michele Evans, published on May 13, 2012.

Chapter 1—The Change

1. "Shadow Play," http://www.wikipedia.org, last edited February 2020 by 169.1.177.234.

2. "All the Way Shay!," Author Unknown, posted by http://www.inspirationpeak.com

3. "Connecting with People—What It Is and Isn't, and Why You Might Find It Hard," Harley Therapy Counseling Blog, last reviewed by Sheri Jacobson, March 21, 2017.

4. "The Difference between a Relationship and a Connection," http://www.theinspirationlifestyle.com, Dan Munro, July 28, 2017.

5. Relationship Compatibility," www.psychalive.org, Lisa Firestone, Ph.D., Relationship Advice, Relationships.

6. "Monarch Mimic—The Copycat Viceroy Butterfly," http://www.thebutterflygrove.com posted by The Butterfly Grove on April 19, 2015.

Chapter 2—Ice

1. "Quick Facts on Icebergs," National Snow and Ice Data Center, http://www.nsidc.org.

2. "Tip of the Iceberg," Definition, *McGraw-Hill Dictionary of American Idioms and Phrasal Verbs*, 2002 by the McGraw-Hill Co., Inc.

3. *Mountain Interval*, "The Road Not Taken," Robert Frost, November 1916, Henry Holt and Company.

4. "Making Peace with the Road Not Taken," Interview of novelist Jesse Browner by Richard Eisenberg, *Forbes*, September 16, 2015.

5. "You Can You Will: 8 Undeniable Qualities of a Winner," Joel Osteen, September 30, 2014, Faith Words (first published January 1, 2014).

6. *Unbreakable*, produced by Barry Mendel, Sam Mercer, M. Night Shyamalan, Release date November 22, 2000.

7. *Glass*, Film series Unbreakable, Director M. Night Shyamalan, quoted by Samuel L. Jackson, Release date January 18, 2019.

Chapter 3—Pure Sweetness

1. "Journey of Life Speech," http://www.youtube.com, Jim Carrey, Maharishi University Graduation. 2014.

2. "Sweetness," http://www.wikipedia.org, last edited March 13, 2020.

3. *No Limits: Blow the CAP Off Your Capacity*, John Maxwell, March 7, 2017, Center Street, Kindle Edition.

Chapter 4—The Lemon

1. "What Makes a Car a Lemon," http://www.carsdirect.com January 27, 2012.

2. "Lemon," htttp://www.Investpedia.com, Julia Kagan, December 18, 2018.

3. "T.D. Jakes—Nothing Just Happens," YouTube video, posted by Michele Evans, published on May 13, 2012.

4. *Boundaries*, Dr. Henry Cloud and Dr. John Townsend, 1992, Zondervan.

Chapter 5—Sweet and Low

1. *(Un)Qualified*, Steven Furtick, pg.26, Multnomah, 2016.

2. "Clueless," 1995 movie, YouTube video posted by Monica Shannon, published on October 30, 2018.

3. "Worry vs. Anxiety—What Is the Difference," Xavia Malcom, Jamaica Hospital Medical Center, November 12, 2019.

4. *Leopoldville, A Tragedy Too Long Secret*, Allan Andrade, originally published in 1997, copyright 2009 by Allan Andrade.

5. *Rocky Balboa*, Rocky Balboa, 2007.

Chapter 6—Adding Splenda to Your Life

1. "What Trees Do Bark Beetle Attack and Can I Get Rid of Them?," http://blog.davey.com, copyright The Davey Tree Expert Co. 2020, May 31, 2018.

2. *Rocky Balboa*, October 6, 2011.

Chapter 7—Equal

1. "Sweeter Than Sugar," by Ellen Crean, CBS News, August 3, 2004.

2. "The Pain of Changing Yourself," by Tony Robbins, YouTube video, published on June 20, 2017, Ernesto Scherer.

3. "Habitat and Adaptation," http://wwf.panda.org, 2020.

4. "13 Signs You're a Judgmental Person (and How to End the Habit), http://www.lonerwolf.com Mateo Sol, 2019.

Chapter 8 — The Formula

1. "What Does It Mean When You See a Cardinal?," http://www. hunting.com, Admin, April 2, 2019.

2. "The Meaning of a Red Cardinal Sighting," http://www.californiapsychics.com, LJ Innes, January 6, 2019.

3. Definition, http://Lexico.com, 2020.

Acknowledgments

First, I want to thank the Lord for the sweetness in my life. Thank you to each person from the experiences in my life. While some are closed chapters, others will forever be present for the duration of my story. Without you, I would not be the man I am today. Sometimes the struggle is the reward. I want to thank Wisdom for his knowledge and his father figure presence in my life. Thank you Direction, for always giving that push when I felt that I could not move forward. To Clarity—from the day you gave birth to me, your love was never doubted. Thank you for giving me vision on days when everything seemed clouded. Thank you, Belief, for the confidence that you give me when I need it most.

Thank you, Shelia, for your countless hours of reading and correction of this incredibly special writing. A special shout out to Little Nick for the lunches and inspiration in the stories written. The cover design only shows a fraction of your brilliant imagination and influential positive energy. To Bubba, thank you for just listening day after day to my endless rambling. I thank the readers for engaging and having the will to change. This book is truly for you.

Hope and Courage. Although we have been through so much together, remember that we did not choose any of this . . . it chose us. These are the blueprints and it was supposed to happen. We have cried, laughed, screamed, but persevered through it all. I am so proud and love you both. Never ever give up. Always remember to lean on each other and the Lord.

Finally, I thank Peace. I was once Fearful, but because of you I am now Fearless. Thank you for showing me what true love is. We ride together, die together. May the sweetness be sweeter, while the sweetest is yet to come!

Made in the USA
Columbia, SC
20 December 2020